# I Know Why The Cheshire Cat Grins: When Shift Happens

## 30 Lessons On Life, Love and Fear

R. Ayité Okyne

# DEDICATION

This is dedicated to the memory of my father James Glover Okyne – an inimitable diplomat and the wind beneath my wings, who taught me equanimity, strength of spirit, and encouraged me to follow my heart.

To my mother, confidante, prayer warrior and best friend, the 'Lady Diana' Elsie Okyne, who gave me my wings, and whose love for me knows no bounds.

# CONTENTS

DEDICATION                                     iii

CONTENTS                                        v

ACKNOWLEDGMENTS                                ix

PREFACE                                         1

WHAT DREAMS MAY COME                            5

HAPPY ENDINGS                                  11

OF LOVE AND FEAR                               17

DON'T DRINK THE POISON                         21

MONEY CAN BUY YOU HAPPINESS                    27

BE INDISPENSABLE                               33

BREAK THE RULES                                37

SILENT SERMONS                                 41

MILE-HIGH SEX IN FIRST                         47

MY STUFF...AND OTHER RIGHTS                    51

GOD ISN'T WHO I THOUGHT SHE WAS                57

WORK SMART, NOT HARD                           65

LIFE IS HARD... AND THEN YOU DIE               69

YOU ARE WHAT YOU EAT                           75

ON ENVY & JEALOUSY                             79

HOUSTON, DO YOU COPY?                          85

MURDER IN THE FIRST                            89

PERFECTION IS OVERRATED                        95

OUR ELASTIC SPIRIT                             99

FRIENDS & LOVERS                                    105

ON PREJUDICE AND FEAR                               115

SMILE, YOU'RE ON LIFE!                              121

SEEING THROUGH ROSE-COLORED GLASSES                 125

LET'S HAVE A KIKI!                                  129

BEYOND BIRTHDAY SUITS                               133

EXPLORE. DREAM. DISCOVER.                           137

RECHARGE & RELOAD                                   141

GETTING TO HAPPY                                    145

REINVENT YOUR STORY                                 151

EPILOGUE                                            159

# ACKNOWLEDGMENTS

My deepest thanks to Todd Ruopp – you know my song even better than I do and sing it to me when I forget the words.

To Prince Ofori-Atta - thanks for believing in my writing and pushing me off the cliff!

My thanks also go to Janna Benge, Dennis Johnson, Angelo Sannasardo, Abyna-Ansaa Adjei and Andre Wood for your candor and advice.

And to my mentors along the way: Jim Randel, Mar Jennings and Ken Goldstein...I am majorly indebted to you. Thanks for pointing the way!

# PREFACE

*"The most beautiful people we have ever known are those who have known defeat, known suffering, known struggle, known loss, and have pulled themselves out of the depths. These people have an appreciation, a sensitivity, and an understanding of life that fills them with compassion, gentleness, and a deep loving concern. Beautiful people do not just happen."*

**- Elisabeth Kübler-Ross**

This book is the result of a countdown I began as I neared my 40th birthday. Like everyone else, my life has had its ups and downs; a dizzying roller-coaster that I have wanted to get off of many times. A major turning point was just after my 11th birthday when my father – a diplomat in the Ghana Foreign Service – lost his job following a military coup d'état. The announcement was made on national radio news, and we happened to be riding together. That was the day life, as I knew it, came crashing down. With no welfare, Social Security or public assistance, we plummeted from a life of privilege to being a hair's breadth away from being homeless. It would take the next 12 years for my father to get a job. During that time we did anything and everything to keep going even when there was no food to put on the table.

Many years later as an adult, far away from home and family, I found myself unemployed for nine months, dependent on the magnanimity of strangers and of friends I seem to be blessed with. But once again, I am now sixteen months and counting into another bout of unemployment, and in between my optimism and cheerfulness, I have my moments of despair, anger and resentment. For someone used to being in control, it's a tough pill to swallow having to accept that there is only so much within my sphere of influence, yet balancing the philosophy that I am the creator of my life.

But I have, on many occasions, taken stock of my life, and it has helped me recalibrate my direction. My overriding desire is to live the life I love and love the life I live. I have always been inspired by beauty, design, experiences and even a sense of fantasy. It is also a great joy to be able to bring people together to share this beauty and joy, because I believe we are all connected in some way, on some spiritual level, regardless of our personal religious or spiritual beliefs.

Whatever your age, I hope you will be able to connect with my experiences in some way and share it with others too. I've been 40 years in the making and I am delighted that I am a work in progress, so

I look forward to hearing from you as well. This could be so much fun!

Now buckle up, grab your reading glasses if you haven't done so already, and start reading! Enjoy!

R. Ayité Okyne

# WHAT DREAMS MAY COME

*"My mission in life is not merely to survive, but to thrive; and to do so with some passion, some compassion, some humor, and some style."*

**– Maya Angelou**

Where do I begin? At the beginning, I suppose…

Well, a little more than a year ago, I came to a crossroads in my life and found myself spiraling out of control until I hit what I thought was rock bottom. Trying to pick myself up by the bootstraps, I began a course in self-evaluation and growth. It was not a program I willingly submitted myself for – trust me, I went in kicking and screaming – but I am grateful for it.

You know that point in your life where you begin to wonder what this is all about? Whether you're doing the right thing; whether you're fulfilling your mission in life? That's where I was. I was torn between following my ambition and aspirations and following what I was beginning to feel I was being called to do: a life of asceticism and spirituality. Honestly, I still haven't found the answer, but I am beginning to see a way to merge the two and still be true to myself.

What is passion? It is that thing that gives you the most joy when you're doing it and you keep coming back to it over and over again. That is where dreams are born. Some of us find our passions and put them on a shelf for the sake of family, a partner or spouse, a job, for life... And some of us go through life trying to find our passions. The problem with trying to find our passions is that we can only find them with our hearts, not our minds. And our minds will invariably overrule our hearts. As mine does. Being a person who is almost equally left- and right- brained, my creative streak is matched by my own analysis of it. And I have been known to overthink things a time or two... (Marie Forleo's *The Secret to Finding Your Passion* is a good read.)

What is mission? It is that thing you feel called to do and it usually involves altruistic motives. That is what gives meaning to our lives. I've always seen my mission as making people happy; making people enjoy their lives. The vehicle has kept changing, but I found that it was always the things that put a smile on someone's face that gave me the most pleasure. When directing an event, I create what I call an 'emotional tunnel' through which I take the audience. An event or show is not just a series of smaller activities strung together but it is an emotional experience from beginning to end. Every word, every ambience change, every sound that made your heart swell or made you gasp, was carefully placed in that emotional tunnel. Just like with my cooking – another of my passions – I really don't cook for myself. I cook for other people's pleasure. It's the looks of surprise, and the moans of pleasure – and even looks of 'this doesn't taste right to me' – that make it all worthwhile.

I guess I have always been a writer. I wrote my first set of short stories and poems at age 11 on my father's hand-me-down typewriter (yes, that was before word processors). And I loved literature at school and took up my mother's love for reading when I learned to read at age 4. But I discovered I had a passion for writing quite by accident when I was telling an acquaintance what I do for a living and added "and I write on the side". A friend of mine who is an editor of a couple of magazines who heard me responded firmly, "No, Ayite, you're a writer". It didn't make sense to me because I didn't necessarily make a living as a writer and I didn't count copywriting or writing for shows as writing. "You have a great way with words and you're a writer".

It wasn't the first time I'd heard that about my writing, but I always thought I hated the process of writing. But then I realized that anytime I came across an interesting scenario, or a subject I was interested in, I would immediately begin crafting how I would write it in my head. So I probably had a passion for writing after all. But it's not just that the activity of clanking on my computer brings me joy, but I enjoy painting ideas and conveying emotions through words (I just wish the thoughts could be 'automagically' put into words!) My quandary is that my passions and mission need to align; I can't have one without the other – they are both necessary for my satisfaction. But my real problem is that I have many passions. So many things excite me! I'm like a kid in a candy store and I want some of everything…and I only have one lifetime…!

Living without a dream is like living life with your eyes wide shut. We become robotic – going through the motions and feeling very little. We are unable to fully experience life because we've put away the very thing that makes life worth living. Every now and then we look up wistfully at the dream we wrapped up in brown paper and tucked out of sight and rationalize why we did the right thing putting it away and come up with ten reasons we can't dust it off and tear off the brown paper. To make up for our guilt, we create surrogate passions: our children, shopping... On the other end of the spectrum, we cover up and numb our pain and shame with smoking, drinking, drugs, sex...

What are your dreams and passions? And what is your mission in life? Take a look at your life: what music do you listen to? What books, magazines or blogs do you read? What activities do you enjoy? What subjects do you like to learn about? What topics make your blood rush? Look for a pattern, but look with your heart not your mind. Ask your closest friends to help you if you like. You might be surprised at what you uncover. Oprah has a useful *Find Your Passion* exercise. Like me, one of your passions might just be under your very nose and you didn't even know it...!

Are you living your own dream, or are you living someone else's dream?

R. Ayité Okyne

# HAPPY ENDINGS

*"Living one day at a time; Enjoying one moment at a time; Accepting hardships as the pathway to peace; Taking, as He did, this sinful world as it is, not as I would have it; Trusting that He will make all things right if I surrender to His Will; That I may be reasonably happy in this life and supremely happy with Him Forever in the next. Amen."*

**– Reinhold Niebuhr**

Trusting and letting go and being assured that you will be okay in the end is a tough thing to do - especially when it comes to major decisions in your life. For people who like me prefer to have things planned, organized and controlled, this is a particularly big one.

My life has been in a state of flux the last few months regarding the next stage of my life. I'm about to graduate, my lease is running out, I still haven't found a job, I can't afford a move back to Los Angeles, and I can't afford to stay in this apartment…lots of decisions to be made, and not enough information to make the decisions; so many things to do and not enough hours in the day to do them, while the clock ticks inexorably to the deadline in a few days…

For a while, I was stressed out about not having enough information to make the decisions I needed to. I couldn't leave and I couldn't stay. I felt caught between a rock and a hard place. It was a choice between the lesser of two evils. This stress began to manifest itself psychosomatically, which is not a cool thing. However, I went to bed one day resolved to feel better the next morning. I had to do one of my "attitude adjustments". In the process, it came to me that I had been in this position many times in my life and things always worked out somehow. Besides, what else could I do? There was no point worrying over elements I could not control. I had to center myself, reaching deep inside to the lesson I have learnt many times: things will be ok. In the end, my friend and angel Stephanie helped me make a choice. Sometimes when we let go, our prayers are answered through channels we didn't realize existed.

I once heard somewhere that if you can't solve it, it isn't a problem - it's reality. It brings to mind the Serenity Prayer and a quote my friend posted on Facebook: "*Sometimes we need to stop planning the future, stop trying to figure out precisely how we feel, stop deciding with our mind what we want our heart to feel. Sometimes we just have to live in the flow.*"

*"I wanted a perfect ending. Now I've learned, the hard way, that some poems don't rhyme, and some stories don't have a clear beginning, middle, and end. Life is about not knowing, having to change, taking the moment and making the best of it, without knowing what's going to happen next. Delicious Ambiguity."*

**- Gilda Radner**

Living in the flow of life is a wonderful way to live, but takes conscious effort on our part to keep us on track, as I had to learn once again. Not living in the flow of life is like trying to swim against the current, cutting against the grain. But living in the flow of life requires a great deal of trust; a complete faith in the process; an unquestioned belief that things will work out just the way they are meant to be - and however that works out...is okay. And like I often say, no situation is intrinsically good or bad - it is the interpretation we put on them that make them good or bad for us.

We are conditioned to believe that we need to make things happen in our life and we want instant results. And as a person who believes in being the author of my life, I am constantly creating the story that is my life. But I also do know that sometimes I need to surrender. The secret and the reality, however, is that by surrendering, we do not abdicate authorship of our life; we do not relinquish control.

Surrender requires a lot more strength than trying to control things that we have no control over. Surrender is not a giving up, but a giving in - giving in to the goodness that is ours for the taking. Surrender is a conscious decision to make room for goodness in our life, and all we are really doing is stepping out of our own way.

# OF LOVE AND FEAR

*"There are two basic forces: fear and love. When we are afraid, we pull back from life. When we are in love, we open to all that life has to offer with passion, excitement and acceptance."*

**- John Lennon**

I often tell people that almost every action we take is motivated by one of two feelings: love or fear. After moving to the United States, I began to notice how much people's lives were dictated by fear. The news is filled with stories about some harm that someone has carried out against another; natural disasters and threats of impending disasters; new medical information that shows how we're all going to die prematurely, and new-fangled elixirs purporting to be the fountain of youth. Indeed, to watch the news dispassionately, one would come to the conclusion that we were all going to hell in a handbasket one way or another.

We live our lives looking out for burglars, pedophiles and sexual predators, backstabbing colleagues, envious friends, ruthless bosses, manipulative spouses, unfaithful partners, greedy corporations, and...I'm out of breath!

In recent years, I've had to work on my fears. I attribute my early success to the fact that I didn't think about fear. I didn't think about failure or repercussions. As a successful business owner at 23, I just did what I did because it seemed right. These days I plan more, consider every angle, every possible consequence and analyze every idea to death, making Hamlet's soliloquy ring true:

*"Thus conscience does make cowards of us all;*
*And thus the native hue of resolution*
*Is sicklied o'er with the pale cast of thought,*
*And enterprises of great pith and moment*
*With this regard their currents turn awry,*
*And lose the name of action."*

In my interactions with people, I've learnt that if you look for negatives, you will find them. If you look for evil, it will find you. This is not to say evil does not exist. I am not so naïve as to suppose bad people do not exist. Indeed, they are everywhere. But I also believe people are innately good and people relate to us based on a host of non-physical, non-observable factors.

If you think of yourself as a radio, you will get the programming available on the particular frequency you choose. I choose to tune in to positive frequencies and minimize the static on my channel.

I think it is courageous to make an informed decision to trust people until given a reason not to. Many times I have had to remind myself how good it feels to trust that I am safe and I will be fine. Life is good.

As a leader, I'd rather be respected and trusted than feared. Leading by fear is a reflection of the leader's own fear. If I put out positive energy, I make my little light shine to make the world a better place and reduce the stress in my life.

Love works better than fear.

# DON'T DRINK THE POISON

*"The weak can never forgive. Forgiveness is the attribute of the strong."*

**- Mahatma Gandhi**

In my country of origin, Ghana, "forgive and forget" is a phrase that is oft-repeated. Ghanaians are generally a non-confrontational people, but I have wondered if the concept of forgiveness has really been understood....

Just about every one of us has been hurt by someone else's words or actions (or inaction). It could be close friends, family or someone we were romantically involved with. Whatever they said or did probably made us hurt, angry, resentful, or betrayed the trust we had in them. In 40 years, I've had my share of them!

To forgive the actions of another means making a conscious choice to release yourself from the anger, resentment and thoughts of revenge. It doesn't just happen. Notice I said releasing yourself, not the other person. Forgiveness does not make what the other person did okay. It does not imply making excuses for what they did. You don't need to tell them they are forgiven to make the forgiveness effective. Forgiveness is a way to rid yourself of negative emotions so you can make room for more positive energy. Forgiveness, in a sense, is more about you than it is about the other person. It is about keeping you in a state of peace.

Forgiveness puts the controls back into your hands. When you forgive, you transition from being a victim to being the hero of your life. You may not have had control over the other person's actions, but you have control over what you do with your emotions and your life after that. Whether you choose to be consumed in the bitterness, resentment and anger caused by someone else, or you choose to disentangle yourself from all of that negativity, the choice is ultimately yours.

For many people, unfortunately, the former is easier to do. The irony is that holding on to the pain is like drinking poison and expecting the other person to die....

Now, forgiving is not a magic wand that makes the pain and hurt go away! Far from it. It is a paradigm shift in your attitude that frees you from the negativity and helps you move on in life with less baggage. The hurt might take some time to heal, but the anger and thoughts of revenge will dissipate. It is surprising how many people carry the resentments of past relationships into new ones and poison them. The resentment is often so deeply buried they do not even know it exists, but it lurks in the shadows, secreting its venom surreptitiously....

Forgiveness does not necessarily mean your relationship with the other person will be reconciled. I have usually made an effort to reconcile those relationships, but reconciliation is not always possible, or even appropriate. It is difficult to reconcile such relationships if the other person accepts no responsibility for their actions that hurt you, or if they refuse to talk to you, or if they died. Forgiveness is not dependent on reconciliation.

Sometimes I have been the one who needs forgiveness from myself. For many years after my father died, I held on to the anger that I was not there when he passed away, as was the rest of the family. With a limited phone network and an almost non-existent ambulance service, I had to physically go and get help. He asked me not to go, but I wasn't about to stand by and do nothing. I even left my wallet and had to come back home – it was the first time I'd done that and I should probably have taken it as a sign... (I still get nervous if I forget my wallet at home). I was at the doctor's when my brother called me saying, "Don't worry about getting help, it's over…"

Many years later I realized I had to forgive myself and eventually did. I still feel the sadness and hurt, but I'm no longer angry. I miss my father and wished I were there when he took his last breath, but I can now embrace that sadness.

My process of forgiving has involved writing a letter addressed to the other person venting my feelings. Once I'm done I read it over (I'm often amazed at my emotions), and with the letter in my hand, I close my eyes and begin deep breathing exercises, breathing in forgiveness and releasing all my anger into the letter. When I feel relaxed and rid of my anger, I burn the letter and watch my anger go up in flames…

Who do you need to forgive today?

# MONEY CAN BUY YOU HAPPINESS

*"Money is only a tool. It will take you wherever you wish, but it will not replace you as the driver."*

**- Ayn Rand**

I'm quite sure you've heard how money cannot buy you happiness, or health, or class, or love, or a host of other things...and in many ways that is true. Having money, in itself, is not a guarantee to happiness. Happiness is not a reward for hard work or earning money; it is a consequence of a series of choices we make each and every day.

Growing up, there was a period of almost ten years when we had no television at home at a time when everyone in the privileged class we once belonged to was getting a VCR. Every night after dinner (when we had dinner) my family and I would sit outside to enjoy the cooler air, chitchatting with neighbors walking by – some would even sit down with us. We'd tell the most insane jokes, tease each other and just have a plain, good old-fashioned good time. Those were some of the best memories of that era of my life. And I think that bond we created sans the technology made us the tight-knit family we are now.

Indeed, having money gives one access to better medical care, better nutrition, bigger, better and faster toys, better education and a whole lot more; however, I have found that the main reason having a lot more money doesn't make people proportionally happier is that they spend the money on the wrong things.

I have friends who swear by 'shopping therapy' - a shopping spree intended to shake them out of a funk or make them feel happier by acquiring some new outfit, gadget or toy. Sometimes it's a dress, other times it's a car...but that's where the problem is.

Buying stuff does not necessarily make one happy - and if it does, the effect is short-lived. I was surprised to find a scholarly document by some faculty of Harvard University, the University of British Columbia and the University of Virginia on the correlation between money and happiness, and it makes for good easy reading, if you are so inclined: *If Money Doesn't Make You Happy Then You Probably Aren't Spending It Right.*

Science has shown that experiences are better than material things at providing happiness, probably because we adapt to new things fairly quickly. How long does the excitement of a new car last? Or the giddiness of having that hot dress? I remember being excited about getting a set of furniture I had wanted for a long time. For days, my heart would just flutter when I got home to see the shiny new furniture decked out in the living room. Soon after, it was just my cool furniture. The reason physical purchases don't satisfy us is that once the excitement wears off, we need another purchase to give us that high again. It becomes a cycle that constantly needs feeding, and, in between highs, we are not as happy.

Experiences, on the other hand, give us a high that we relive any time we recollect or recount the experience. I had my first parasailing experience in the Bahamas some years ago. I was very nervous about it but I did it anyway. Once I got over the roller coaster feel from the winds, I began to take in the awesomeness of the views and the whole experience. High up in the air, I noticed the calm and stillness and couldn't help but feel like I was getting a glimpse of the Universe's point of view. The waves lapped languidly at the shore, tiny people were going about their business, fish were swimming in the clear water... and I was above it all, with nary not a sound but my breathing and my heartbeat. It was an incredible spiritual moment, which I count in my top 5. I also distinctly remember the exhilaration of being at the controls and flying a plane for the first time; the headiness of being taken by helicopter from Van Nuys to Long Beach, CA on my birthday... for dinner, mind you... To this day, I get excited thinking about those experiences or telling people about them - and of course, I don't need to be asked twice, and I'll be bursting to tell the story again. Like I just did.

In a recent study of more than one thousand Americans, it was found that those who purchased experiences (57%) derived greater happiness from their purchase than those who purchased physical items (34%). We anticipate the experiences and remember them much more than physical things - and that is the secret to happiness. Well, at least one of them. Things bring us happiness only when we use them, but experiences make us happy when we think about them.

So I've learnt that money can buy you happiness. You just have to spend it on the right things...

Next time you need an 'upper', or you feel the urge to shop to make you happy, consider taking a cooking class, or going to a concert, or learning a new skill. You'll be glad you did and you will prolong the effect of your happiness.

That's why the Cheshire cat grins....

# BE INDISPENSABLE

*"To maintain your independence, you must always be needed and wanted"*

**- Robert Green, The 48 Laws of Power**

In my first job - an unofficial and unpaid internship - I learned very early on the importance of being indispensable. I didn't set out with that intention - it was actually a by-product of something else. I started out with the task of organizing an abandoned file room - a task I finished in 3 days, much to the dismay of my supervisor. I kept asking for more things to do. What I wanted was more responsibility to feed my need to be important. I figured I was smart, and I could do more, so I asked for more to keep me busy (*sometimes I believe in as many as six impossible things before breakfast*). Within three months, I had a title, and in six months, I was convening meetings (and still not getting paid).

With my increased trust and responsibility came even more responsibility. At age 22, it was exhilarating to be coordinating a major international arts festival spread across 6 cities and 26 venues. I enjoyed being in the thick of it all and being the go-to person as the third-in-command. With an eagle-eye view of all the operations (and having gone through all of that information in the file room), I was the repository of all kinds of information and was given considerable authority. But things came to a head for me one day in a very embarrassing way. One of my special responsibilities was for VIPs and heads of state. I had to meet a VIP at the airport and escort her to the main festival city two hours away. I had been awake for at least 48 hours straight, had made three return trips of the two-hour journey in that period and the flight was delayed. I fell into a deep sleep at the wheel while I waited and only woke up hours after the flight had arrived! Needless to say, this personality felt slighted and I was totally mortified. I had taken on more than I could handle in my enthusiasm and everyone was happy to give me more responsibility - and I botched it.

But it showed me how much power I wielded. Actually, it is the 11th Law of Power in Robert Greene's 48 Laws of Power: "*Learn to keep people dependent on you.*" I did the same at another job, going the extra mile. It helped save me through several waves of downsizing, and after I left, they went through three replacements.

Being indispensable puts incredible power in your hands. Greene says, "To maintain your independence, you must always be needed and wanted". Fortunately, it doesn't apply only to work situations. You can use it in your everyday interactions: whatever you do, do it better than anyone else can. The more of those you can do, the more dependent people are on you and the more independent you become. In a subtle way, you gain the upper hand, and are potentially in the position to get people to do what you want done without having to force them to do it.

What is your secret to power? Who are you dependent on, and who is dependent on you? Where is the balance of power?

# BREAK THE RULES

*"If I had a world of my own, everything would be nonsense. Nothing would be what it is because everything would be what it isn't. And contrary-wise; what it is, it wouldn't be, and what it wouldn't be, it would. You see?"*

**– Alice, Alice in Wonderland**

As a young boy, I was rather obsessed with following the rules and doing everything right. For me it was avoiding the embarrassment of disapproval or punishment. My mother was quite the disciplinarian. I needed to have the approval of my parents at all times and if they so much as looked at me the wrong way, my very soul was crushed. So when I was punished for anything I'd done at home or at school, I would be very mad at myself for being wrong. I considered punishment to be beneath me and that was why I followed the rules.

I still think punishment is abhorrent and a parking ticket has been known to ruin my day and the next three as well. But this piece is not about public laws and organizational rules. It's about the unwritten rules in life we feel compelled to obey because that is what we understand society expects of us. We have rules that govern what we wear, how our relationships should work, what roles we play, how we should feel and myriad other aspects of our life. We effectively become drones, accepting our lot in life and the status quo because that's the thing to do.

In many ways, my adult life has been one of being unconventional: I chose to pursue a liberal arts education against my parents' desires; I chose to be an entrepreneur instead of getting a regular job; I left my country to settle in a country I knew no one in, and started a new life; I left a full time job I despised – although it gave me stability – to pursue another degree, precipitating a move to a state across the country.

It does feel like looking in from the outside sometimes, but I won't have it any other way. In the words of Robert Heinlein: *"I am free because I know that I alone am morally responsible for everything I do. I am free, no matter what rules surround me. If I find them tolerable, I tolerate them; if I find them too obnoxious, I break them. I am free because I know that I alone am morally responsible for everything I do."*

I prefer to chart my own course in life and find myself constantly questioning conventions; essentially dancing to the beat of a different drum. It would be amazing to find out how much of our lives are dictated by convention. Breaking those rules, in my experience, has been liberating in the long run.

Take a moment to think about the things you do each day and ask yourself why you do those things. Why do they have to be that way? Is that the only way it can be done? Just thinking about those questions in an objective and dispassionate manner can be quite revealing. If done correctly and honestly, you will feel uncomfortable with what you come up with and will realize that even what you think is 'right' is only right because you've been conditioned to think that is what 'right' looks like.

Get out of your comfort zone.
Break some rules.
Free your mind.

# SILENT SERMONS

*"It takes a lot of courage to release the familiar and seemingly secure, to embrace the new. But there is no real security in what is no longer meaningful. There is more security in the adventurous and exciting, for in movement there is life, and in change there is power."*

**- Alan Cohen**

On a recent trip back home, I decided to put myself to use and help my mother de-clutter her home – and in particular, a certain wall unit - à la Oprah. You see, mother – bless her heart – loves to keep all sorts of objects as souvenirs and mementoes of bygone years. In this piece of furniture, I found all sorts of things I had no idea she had – class registers from when she ran a pre-school (ten years earlier, mind you!), circulars, baby shower and engagement party favors and so much more. As I carefully wrapped and boxed away the fragile objects it seemed like there had been more that I boxed than this cabinet was capable of holding. When it came to the things in the 'throw away' pile, my heart went out to this cabinet! It was incredible what it had had to contain all these years...

The cabinet, along with the furniture in the house, holds a very dear place in the story of my family. They were a symbol of overcoming after living a very frugal lifestyle below the poverty line (even for Africa). Changing the furniture, for us, was a new start; the beginning of a new life. We were once again able to buy furniture, albeit cheap, but it was very symbolic - and custom-made, I'll have you know! As I unloaded this piece of family history, none of this was lost on me. I remembered how we proudly picked out curios to display in it. It also had a lot of storage, so it was very useful for tucking away the not-so-nice stuff we didn't want guests seeing.

With everything emptied out of it, the cabinet seemed like a ghost of its former self: sagging shelves, peeling veneer, doors that fell off their hinges and joints coming apart. I asked some strapping young men to come and help me take it out of the house, but that was unnecessary – the cabinet collapsed with one push. Emptied of all its baggage, the cabinet gave up the ghost like a house of cards. It was a very sad but poignant moment.

It made me think of the parallels in our own lives. We accumulate a lot of baggage over the years and struggle under their weight, but we keep chugging along like 'the little engine that could'. We hold on to a lot of emotions, experiences, and perceptions, both negative and positive. Sometimes, this spills over into our physical lives in the form of clutter. We jealously guard them, straining under their pressures, but refusing to let go.

Sometimes it helps to remove ourselves from our attachments and objectively purge ourselves of everything, keeping only that which we need for the way forward. It always feels good to know we can go back to some object or the memory of an event for comfort, but we should pick wisely. We need to occasionally take inventory of our lives and run an audit to make us leaner and lighter for the journey of life. This may mean changing our attitudes, correcting self-defeating behaviors or forgiveness – forgiving others who may have offended us, but also, believe it or not, forgiving ourselves. We can only love ourselves unconditionally after we forgive ourselves for whatever it is we blame ourselves for. We can't love another person without loving ourselves first. And we are surprised when our human relationships are painful...?

Carrying around our heavy baggage affects not just us as individuals, but also everyone else who shares our life in some way. Without realizing it, and by default, we force others to carry our baggage just as we carry others' baggage, whether we realize it or not. That is why sometimes when we feel our loads are too heavy, it's because of the other people's loads we share.

Whatever your clean out is — whether it is forgiveness, changing your attitude to someone or a situation — renewing your spirit makes room for newness and positivity in your life. As much as it hurts to let go of things that have, in some twisted way, provided comfort in the past, it is necessary for our growth and forward movement.

Unclench your fists. Let go.
Release. Submit to the now.

This is what I learnt in the moment that cabinet folded up with almost no help in my mother's living room. It no longer had to be strong and keep it together. But it had to go to make room for new furniture. Look into your life and find those things you're holding on to that do not serve any real purpose. Release them so you can embrace your new life.

Remember, to live the life you love, you must love the life you live!

# MILE-HIGH SEX IN FIRST

*Sex is full of lies. The body tries to tell the truth. But, it's usually too battered with rules to be heard, and bound with pretenses so it can hardly move. We cripple ourselves with lies.*

**- Jim Morrison**

Sex. The very thought of it is enough to conjure up visions of hedonistic abandon and heights of incredible ecstasy... or not.

It is amazing how sex has changed for me over the years. Time was when sex had but one objective: the surreptitious foray through the nether regions to reach the intoxicating heights of Mt. Olympus - the mount of the gods - if only for an all-too-brief moment. It was a speedy race to the top to reach the Holy Grail and an avalanche right back down that left you flushed, out of breath, and feeling less than satiated.

Like many young people, we were left wondering why there was so much secrecy, mystery and much ado about sex. Yes, it was great, but only very briefly, really. And what was so wrong about it that made it such an awful subject in polite company or at the dinner table? Somehow the clandestine nature of the subject of sex lent credence to its allure.

Sometimes I wonder how sex today would be if I'd had lots of early experience. In many ways I am still learning so much about it. You would think that at my age I would know everything about my body and about sex. The real beauty is that I am still learning, and each new revelation leaves me with a smile on my face.

I find it sad that many times, sex is seen as something we do to another person, or something that is done to us. That is sad. It should be an act of mutual participation, where each partner's aim is to please and be pleased. Without that essential ingredient, it is nearly impossible for both parties to derive optimal benefit from being together.

What I do know is that there are different kinds of sex. Sex is like nature. You can have earthquakes, hurricanes, snow flurries, thunderstorms, drizzles, breezes and sometimes stillness. Sometimes several happen in succession. Sometimes it's good, sometimes it isn't. But most importantly, it is about the spiritual connection that can take place in the process. Sex is more than a genital experience. It is a spiritual experience that echoes the Biblical reference of two becoming one. It is one of those rare moments where bodies and spirits collide. A sexual encounter disconnected from a spiritual one is like flying coach when you could be flying First Class.

A spiritual sexual encounter requires both parties to be present and committed to the 'process'. It involves tuning in to the frequency of the other person as well as yourself, and interpreting the very subtle signals you give and receive. Consciously take in what you see, what you smell, what you taste, what you feel, how it feels...that is when it takes on a life of its own and the two of you take a journey that is not predetermined by either party. The only agenda is the present moment. That is when sex is no longer about the orgasm as much as it is about a series of moments of a certain shared intimacy. Each encounter is a new adventure, blending the tried-and-tested with new areas of exploration and a conscious abandonment to the moment.

I have found that a spiritual sexual encounter leaves me satiated and basking in the afterglow for days afterwards and doesn't leave me craving more (not for the moment, at least). It has taken me a while to learn the import of that, but I have also had to unlearn a lot of what I picked up growing up. Sex can be an incredibly beautiful experience, but you need to learn to 'unlimit' yourself and realize that really, there are no rules.

You are the rule.

# MY STUFF...AND OTHER RIGHTS

*"Ownership attaches an emotion and an expectation. Expectation leads to conflict in most every situation"*

**-Ken Goldstein, The Way of The Nerd**

It's amusing to watch kids, even in pre-school, fight over toys crying, "It's mine, it's mine!" tugging at whatever toy got both their attention and their right of ownership. Due to some very interesting socialization process, we teach kids a sense of ownership. It's my toy/my bed/my mummy/my whatever it is. As adults, we extend that to people as well.

I am - as you might imagine - very much into the finer things in life. I've always been. I've always been about exclusivity and being unique. Even as a boy, my mother always knew to get me something that was different from whatever she got for my brothers. It had to be mine - I wouldn't be caught dead in anything that even remotely looked like someone else's!

But a strange thing happened to me as I grew up. Years ago, I woke up one day to find that my car had been broken into in the driveway of my house. The stereo was taken and some other bits and bobs that I can't remember. I felt violated and angry, and also very vulnerable.

15 years later it seems like a non-event. Did that burglary have an effect on who I am today? I doubt it. Reflecting on the events of the day and my emotions in response, I realized that these things taken away from me were just stuff. Yes, I was upset and felt vulnerable, but it was because someone else had taken my stuff. Although the gaping hole where my car stereo had been ripped out reminded me of the atrocious act (yes, I'm being dramatic!), I made my peace when I disconnected myself from my ownership of the physical object. I had to let go.

My friend Ken Goldstein puts it very well in his new book *"The Way of The Nerd"*: *"Ownership attaches an emotion and an expectation. Expectation leads to conflict in most every situation."*

We extend our sense of entitlement and ownership to our relationships as well and consider our romantic partners as 'ours', and as a result, a breakup is so much more painful not because of the fact that we loved (and probably still love) them, but because we feel they had no right to take away what we considered ours. And this is amplified if a third party was involved. We cannot claim ownership of the people in our life.

During an amicable but no less painful breakup, my ex and I agreed to 'release' each other. We'd talked about loving someone enough to let them go. For many weeks, I went through the pain of post-breakup. One day, I realized that what I was really mourning was the wonderful moments we'd had; the deep bond of friendship that would no longer be the same; the nights of catching up that we'd no longer have. I also feared the prospect of being alone, paralyzed by the knowledge that I would eventually have to face the terrorizing maze of dating after such a long time. I acknowledged that I still loved them – loved them enough to release them with no anger, malice or ill intent, but instead with love, gentleness and blessing. I did cry because it was over, but it felt good to be comforted by the fact that I'd been blessed with love and now, fond memories.

This may sound like quantum theory, but a thought that brings the concept of ownership sharply into focus is that we cannot lose something we do not own. We are merely stewards of whatever we have. But even more importantly, no one will steal something we do not own. It's like a reverse self-fulfilling prophecy: if you don't own it, no one will steal it. Isn't that freeing? For me, it makes me sleep easier at night without fearing that my stuff will be taken. The stuff is replaceable. The stuff I paid for, I paid for the use of them while I'm here. I came into this world kicking and screaming and with absolutely nothing - not even the clothes on my back. And I will leave without any of it as well.

I like my fine stuff. But I own none of it.

# GOD ISN'T WHO I THOUGHT SHE WAS

*"It is I who am the light which is above them all. It is I who am the all. From me did the all come forth, and unto me did the all extend. Split a piece of wood, and I am there. Lift up the stone, and you will find me there."*

**- Jesus, The Gospel of Thomas**

It just hit me the other day that God isn't who I thought He was. I'm not sure what went wrong along the way, but I was given a heavy dose of the wrong God. And no, it is not because someone decided to misinform me - because everyone that has crossed my spiritual path has had the best of intentions.

There was a time I felt I would never be able to measure up to God's standards as a Christian. It didn't matter that I was taught that Jesus Christ had died for my sins once and for all. (But then, if He did, why did I still have to strive to be good if all my sins were paid for in advance?) It was a very frustrating time for me as I battled with my nature and my beliefs.

## God Then...

I was raised Catholic, went to a Catholic preparatory school, became the Catholic Chapel Prefect in high school and nearly went to seminary. I joined the Scripture Union at school, started a youth group in my parish, organized Bible study, gospel concerts...I was 'on fire'.

Unfortunately, religion has covered all of the simple beauty of the love of God with a lot of ritual, dogma and rules. I used to believe in a God that was watching everything you did, waiting to punish you now or later for eternity, but with a veneer of love thrown in for good measure. The God I used to believe in was to be feared. I had to believe in Him, or else....

God was this phantasmagoric being that lived way beyond the clouds, beyond my sight, with an eye on me at all time checking on everything I did with a tally sheet that He would refer to when I died, to decide if He would let St. Peter unlock the gates of heaven for me, or throw me into Lucifer's hell. Scripture verses such as 2 Thessalonians 1:8-9 *In flaming fire taking vengeance on them that know not God, and that obey not the gospel of our Lord Jesus Christ: Who shall be punished with everlasting destruction from the presence of the Lord, and from the glory of his power* (KJV) kept me in terror of this vengeful God who would have His justice if I didn't do as he said, exactly how He wanted me to.

## God Now...

I began a search some years ago that made me see God in a whole new light and the vision is incredibly stunning. I have no less fervor now than I did then, but my focus is now more inward than outward.

My slant is more spiritual than religious. The outward appearances of self-righteousness no longer impress me. I still love the pomp and pageantry, but am less impressed. I realize that the God I came to believe in had been commercialized, dressed up, and paid mere lip service. Indeed, the God I came to believe in was no more than a human fabrication, created to control people, and very successfully too.

I found that men had tried to put God in a handy little box that made it easier for them to comprehend Him. What happened was that we put limitations on God. We ascribed human emotions and thought processes to Her, and related to Him on that level. Yes, the switching of pronoun gender is intentional! We assigned a gender that made God male because that was what a patriarchal society could accept, and our language could only support a male or female gender. The God I knew before was nothing but a human construct, made in the image of man. How ironic: God creates man in Her own image and man, in turn, recreates God in his lowly image...

Now, more than ever, I realize God is love. Now, more than ever, I feel God within me, and I feel a part of God. Now I understand that with God's gift of free will, I am a co-creator with Her each waking moment. God works with me, in me, through me, as me.... Like the fruit of the vine, I am an extension of God and - dare I say it - I am a piece of God! To fully experience God, I have to be open-minded and refrain from projecting my human limitations unto The One Spirit, and yes, let God be God.

God sees me no differently than He sees you and neither should I. God wants us to love Her of our own free will and not because of some threat of fire and brimstone. God, by whatever name we refer to Her, is not Christian. Neither is He Buddhist or Muslim or Hindu. God isn't black or white or brown; She isn't straight or gay or bisexual: God just is. Religion pits us one against the other, creating an environment of "us versus them", each arrogantly trying to claim exclusive rights to God. There is more than enough God to go around! A statement made by a pastor in the movie *Children of*

*God* put this in stark perspective for me: *"We have to give people something to hate. It brings them together...."* Now let that sink in for a moment.... It is never so openly acknowledged, but isn't that what religion tends to do? Sadly, it is people who create the problem, adding all the fluff to a simple spirituality, turning it into a codified system of worship and organization called "religion".

There are no exclusions in God's love. No ifs, buts or whys. God's love has no strings attached; no conditions. My faith is no longer determined by scriptural texts conveniently selected by humans to suit their purposes. God's love for me is not predicated upon anything I do or don't do. I cannot earn God's divine grace. God's love is – get this – unconditional! I no longer beat myself up for not being able to measure up to man-made rules made in God's name - She loves me just the way I am. My mission is to spread His love in everything I do - God working in me, through me, as me.

I have learned that God really doesn't care if you call Her Allah, the Universe, Mother Nature, God, Adi Purush, Waheguru, Elohim, Ewurade, Onyankopon, use a male or female pronoun, or paint Him white, black or brown, with long hair and a beard, or bald. What God does care about is that you love your neighbor as yourself. You cannot claim to love God if you are selective about which neighbor you will love, or under what conditions you will love them. Truth be told, you cannot love your neighbor if you don't love yourself. It's a simple as that!

I now have a new sense of freedom and an entirely new perspective.

## Prayer of St. Francis

*Lord, make me an instrument of Your peace.*
*Where there is hatred, let me sow love.*
*Where there is injury, pardon.*
*Where there is doubt, faith.*
*Where there is despair, hope.*
*Where there is darkness, light.*
*Where there is sadness, joy.*

*O Divine Master,*
*Grant that I may not so much seek to be consoled, as to console;*
*To be understood, as to understand;*
*to be loved, as to love.*
*For it is in giving that we receive.*
*It is in pardoning that we are pardoned,*
*And it is in dying that we are born to Eternal Life.*

# WORK SMART, NOT HARD

*"Progress isn't made by early risers. It's made by lazy men trying to find easier ways to do something."*

**— Robert A. Heinlein**

Some days I just want to be lazy. There's no nice way to put it. But I own it and make no apologies for it. Today is one of them. And guess what? I'm playing Bruno Mars' *The Lazy Song*!

The older I've grown, the less I want to work – the hard kind, at least. Don't get me wrong: I love the work I do and I'm a very hands-on person, but I've paid some dues and am throttling back. Years ago, it was cool to work hard, doing the things I loved to do for just a pittance; right now - not so much.

Many of you might be familiar with Pareto's 80/20 principle – you get 80% of your work done with 20% of your resources. I want to use as little energy as possible to get the most results. It's efficiency, plain and simple. For me, it is a transition from being effective to being efficient; or better still: effective and efficient.

Effectiveness is the easy part. As a young business owner barely out of my teens, it was important to me that I be in the trenches with my crew. That was my leadership style, and besides, everyone was older than I was, and I felt uncomfortable barking orders to them. It didn't help that I was a perfectionist. It was easier to do it myself and get it right, sometimes. But with a growing scope of responsibilities, I couldn't be everywhere at the same time. That is where mentoring, delegation, and succession planning come in.

To work smarter, one should focus on the big stuff; things that will make the most impact - the rest will follow. In the same vein, you have to manage your time differently - spending more time on the things that will produce the biggest results, not necessarily the most aesthetically pleasing. Not every battle needs to be fought to win the war: some are more crucial than others, so pick your battles.

I'm not 100% motivated 100% of the time, and I'm pretty sure the same goes for you as well. Motivation comes and goes like waves - when I have a nice big wave, I ride it all the way. After it's crested, I don't need to spin my wheels because I'll be spending a lot more of my energy for little return. Besides, another wave will certainly come again; the downside, however, is that I never know when the next one will be, or how long it will last. But if you're resourceful enough, I'm sure you can make your own waves...

In my experience, there's almost always a better way to do any given task, and I'm always looking for that. I don't want to spend energy I don't need to be spending. Don't restrict yourself to a method just because that's the way it's always been. In several jobs I've had, my supervisors would get frustrated with all the 'why' questions I had. But I needed to know why I was doing any given task in the context of the whole. That perspective also gives me ideas to streamline processes.

There are two kinds of people: those who work hard and those who work smart. Those who work hard measure their success in the number of hours they work and hope it reflects in their paycheck. Those who work smart measure their success in how much discretionary time they have available. That's the kind of guy I want to be! I'm sure many of you were either told or made to believe that you had to 'pay your dues' in hard work, and the only reason for that was 'because you have to'. No you don't!

I have no interest in working hard only to find that I don't have the time to enjoy the fruits of my labor. I want to have a work-life balance that keeps me excited, energized and enthusiastic. I want to work in my retirement because I love what I do and it keeps me young.

Take a moment to think today what message you're sending to kids by your words and actions about life and work. Are you teaching them to work hard or work smart?

I don't know about you, but as for me, the only thing I'm going to work hard at... is working smart.

# LIFE IS HARD... AND THEN YOU DIE

*"Be thankful for what you have; you'll end up having more. If you concentrate on what you don't have, you will never, ever have enough"*

**— Oprah Winfrey**

Life is hard. And then you die. The title of this piece may sound rather pessimistic, but it's not. Perhaps it got your attention. (And for the technical nit-pickers: forgive my use of 'hard' instead of 'difficult' in this post - it just sounds better here!)

It's often said that the two things that are certain in life are death and taxes - let me add a third: tough times. Everyone goes through some tough times regardless of one's station in life, financial stability, or optimism. I know I've had my share of them. It is very easy in life to get frustrated because sometimes things don't work out as we expect.

In a green room event I attended with Jim Randel, author of *The Skinny On...* series, he mentioned how important it is for people to recognize and accept that in any endeavor, problems can and will arise. Sometimes anything and everything that can go wrong will go wrong.

I wanted to have kids by 30 and that didn't happen, and as much I have mourned that loss on occasion, I have made my peace with it and enjoy all cute sweet kids that somehow seem to adore me. I wanted to have a flawless dinner party last night with my friends, but I forgot the side of marmalade-glazed green beans until it was time for dessert…and no one missed it but me (yes, I did it again).

So how does one reconcile my philosophy of 'life is good' with 'life is hard'? Therein lies the rub: life is a contradiction in terms. The way to experience 'life is good' is to first acknowledge 'life is hard'. By recognizing that problems can and will arise, problems become par for the course, and are less likely to throw us off kilter, or heaven forbid, throw us in a conniption!

Acknowledging that problems can arise helps us plan ahead, and put controls in place that will help avoid the situation altogether, or mitigate the consequences if the situation cannot be avoided. Beware of becoming such a control freak and anally-retentive that the problems appear bigger than they really are. That would defeat the purpose.

I used to work for someone who was so obsessed with perfection that I could swear he actually willed the problems into reality by being so focused on what problems could arise!

It works similarly to the Law of Attraction, which states that by focusing on positive or negative thoughts, one can bring about positive or negative results – like attracts like. But when you're stuck in a rut, when you're desperate, when you're scared and trying to find a way out, it's difficult to see the positive side of things. When you feel like you're drowning, you first thought isn't "Let me drink as much of this chlorinated water as I can – people would kill for a drop of this water!" Most likely not, when you perceive your life to be in danger.

But perception is what gets in the way. Just like in the drowning example, we forget our bodies would float if we didn't fight so much. Instead of focusing on relaxing and floating, we resort to fearing the worst and fight to avoid the thing we fear could happen. It then becomes a self-fulfilling prophecy.

The way I see it, life is good. I wouldn't know how good it was if there were none of the not-so-good moments. Just like I wouldn't know light if there were no darkness. Just like there would be no good without evil (and this is by no means an endorsement for evil!).

The hardships and frustrations in our life keep us grounded and keep us from taking the magnificence of our lives for granted. Focusing on what is wrong with our life situation instead of how good our life is, misses the point entirely. It is like looking at a white sheet of paper with an ink stain on it and seeing only the little stain -forgetting that there is a lot more white around the stain. It is all about perception. No situation is inherently good or bad - it is the interpretation that we give to it that makes it appear good or bad to us.

Life is hard and then you die. Yes, maybe. But remember to live the life you love and love the life you live. And count your blessings. You'll be surprised how many you have. That is Life - Inspired.

# YOU ARE WHAT YOU EAT

*If you really want to make a friend, go to someone's house and eat with him... the people who give you their food give you their heart.*

*– Cesar Chavez*

I don't always eat a balanced, healthy diet each day, especially with my self-confessed sweet-tooth cravings, and we all know that butter and bacon make anything taste better! But I approach my diet more from a perspective of moderation. I don't cut out huge swaths of food types or try to stay on a strict regimented diet. For an acknowledged foodie like me, that doesn't work. Neither is it fun. I believe my diet should be sensible and work with my lifestyle as well.

However, a friend of mine gave me a new and insightful perspective on my eating habits. He said, "Make sure everything that goes into your body benefits it in some way." In other words, if it isn't helping your body in some way, that is extra work you're giving your body and you'll pay for it later. In this school of thought, your diet is not based on calorie counts or low-carbs, or whatever the current fad is, but on the nutritional value of what you're eating. Is it helping you live longer, live better, sleep better, run faster or have better sex? If it isn't doing anything positive for your body, take a second look at it.

My weight has jumped as my body changed from the skinny teenager I was, to the more filled-out version I am today. I have noticed my metabolism slow down, but I've tried to keep it up with exercise and activity. Call me vain, but I liked my body better when it was 5 lbs. lighter....

Every few months, I do a 'refrigerator and pantry audit' to assess what kinds of foods I have and also to purge myself of negative net-value food that I might have stealthily introduced over time (yes, I do that too). This also gives me the opportunity to stock up on more positive net-value foods. You might want to do that too...

If you are what you eat, what am I? Food for thought...

*Did you ever stop to taste a carrot? Not just eat it, but taste it? You can't taste the beauty and energy of the earth in a Twinkie.*

— Astrid Alauda

# ON ENVY & JEALOUSY

*"Love sees sharply, hatred sees even more sharply, but jealousy sees the sharpest, for it is love and hate at the same time..."*

**- Arabic saying**

I think I am pretty weird when it comes to jealousy, especially in the context of relationships. I know many people who subscribe to the thoughts of St. Augustine: *"He that is not jealous is not in love."* I have a fundamental problem with that because of what it suggests. The quotation that somewhat expresses my sentiments is by François, Duc de La Rochefoucauld: *"In jealousy there is more self-love than love."*

Jealousy involves three parties: you, a person you see as a rival, and something or somebody you desire. With jealousy, your focus is more on the object of desire than your rival. When you are jealous, you are afraid you could lose that thing or person to your rival because of an inadequacy you perceive yourself to have. Jealousy is fear. In a sense, it says "if I can't have him, you shouldn't either", which connotes some element of malice. But more importantly, it says, "I think you are better qualified than I to have the object of my desire", which connotes a feeling of inadequacy and a lack of self worth. The other side of the coin, where a person expects to be jealously guarded also suggests feelings of insecurity since the person's feelings of self-worth are predicated upon someone else's actions.

Envy, on the other hand, as Aristotle describes it, is *"pain at the good fortune of others"* even though it does not take anything away from what you already have. It is one of the 'seven deadly sins'. Envy is when you wish you had, or want something that someone else has, or when you think: "why should they have this and not me?", but there is no impending loss. With envy, because the focus is more on the rival than the object of desire, if that good fortune went to someone else, the feeling of envy would die out. Envy occurs when your standard of self-worth is defined by how it compares to others. Taken further, it can be the dislike of another's well-being or good fortune because they are not deserving of it, in our sole (and not so humble) opinion.

I don't consider myself jealous. Indeed my love has been called into question on occasion because of my lack of jealous inclinations. But I have realized that I cannot hold on to another's affections – like an egg, if you don't hold it tight enough, you will lose it; if you hold on too tightly you will break it. Jealousy also engenders suspicion, which in turn erodes the foundation of trust that relationships are built on, and eventually, like a house of cards, the relationship comes crashing down. Suspicion makes one look for reasons to question another's loyalty, and, in most cases, you will eventually find what you've been looking for – akin to a self-fulfilling prophecy.

I have learnt that while I hope my relationship with the person I love will last forever, I cannot control the other person's feelings or actions. I am with them because they choose to be with me and that is my blessing and good fortune. I cannot say I will not be hurt, disappointed and even angry if they decided not to be with me, but I will understand that it is their prerogative and sole right to decide who they will be with; a right I have as well.

I think benign envy is par for the course because of our innate desires and the pursuit of life, liberty and happiness. We will always see someone with something that we wished we had. I know I do. Will I cut them for it? Absolutely not. I will be happy for them but it will spur me on to be in the position to get what they have that I like.

I can understand envy, but I despise jealousy in any form because it is a sign of weakness and tells me so much about the person it is coming from. Jealousy, in my opinion, is not attractive and screams "Extra Baggage – Beware!" and all its attendant abandonment issues, and I shy away from such energy. But I also realize that for many people, they need to see some element of jealousy to make them feel wanted and desired.

There is an Arab saying that goes: *"Love sees sharply, hatred sees even more sharply, but jealousy sees the sharpest, for it is love and hate at the same time..."*

Something to think about.

# HOUSTON, DO YOU COPY?

*"Too often we underestimate the power of a touch, a smile, a kind word, a listening ear, an honest compliment, or the smallest act of caring, all of which have the potential to turn a life around."*

**— Leo Buscaglia**

Have you ever been with someone who talks your ear off and you can't shimmy in a word edgewise? I have, and more times than I care to remember.

But I do enjoy listening to people's stories - stories of triumph, joy, sadness or pain. Admittedly, sometimes I hear more than I need to know or even want to know, but it's par for the course. By listening, I learn so much about human nature and the world around me, and, most importantly, about the person who's speaking. I pick up on their attitudes and values, what's important to them, and their worldview.

I once heard a speaker talking about the difference between hearing and listening and I found it rather fascinating. It is easy to hear what someone says without really listening to what they have to say. Listening requires active participation - hearing doesn't. You can hear just by virtue of the fact that you have working ears. Listening involves paying attention to words, inflections and tone, as well as reading between the lines to find emotion, subtext, motive, what is said, and even what is not said. I have found that I am pretty good at picking out word choices and what is not said. Listening is discovering what is really being said.

Listening requires a genuine desire and interest in what is being said and in the person talking. It requires a willingness to make a meaningful connection with a speaker and their message, and go along on a journey with them. Effective listening will involve keeping an open mind and reserving your judgment, focusing on the message, being engaged in the conversation, and avoiding the urge to be defensive (even if you feel attacked). Yes, to really listen, you need to shut up.

Many of us at some point have been around someone who just seems to love the sound of their own voice. Those situations might have left us wanting to find an excuse just to get away because we felt we were not being recognized - our thoughts were not needed, wanted, or important enough to the other person.

Each one of us wants to feel acknowledged - and listening is a good way to make people feel acknowledged. Everyone wants to feel like they're being heard - listened to. By communicating through the simple act of listening that whatever the other person has to say is important to you, you communicate that the other person is important to you. This creates a shared bond that we all crave and does wonders for all kinds of relationships.

Make someone feel important today. You'll be glad you did.

# MURDER IN THE FIRST

*"While I thought that I was learning how to live, I have been learning how to die...."*

**- Leonardo da Vinci**

Today, I learned that a gentleman in our church took his life – committed suicide, to wit. I hardly knew the man, indeed, I have no recollection of his face, but for some reason I was weighed down with grief throughout Mass.

Just back from a pilgrimage to Jerusalem, the priest's sermon focused on the 'uneasy truces' that exist in the Holy Land. I couldn't help wondering what uneasy truces this man had had to deal with in his life; what crosses he had to bear.

What great cowardice leads one to the precipice and pushes right through into the yawning chasm of such awesome courage to take one's own life? The irony here is that the victim and the perpetrator are one and the same.

The word 'suicide' comes from the Latin word *suicidium*, derived from *sui caedere*, which means 'to kill oneself'.

Suicide attempts are said to occur for a number of reasons including depression, shame, guilt, desperation, physical pain, emotional pressure, anxiety, financial difficulties, gay shame or other undesirable situations. They are often a permanent solution to a temporary, or otherwise manageable, situation.

The person who takes their life chooses to end their problems in death, but in doing so, creates further problems for those they leave behind. Sadly, many of them die not knowing how much they were loved!

According to the Word Health Organization, about 1 million people complete suicide each year – more than the people who die in wars. But more disconcerting is the fact that 10 to 20 million people attempt suicide each year! That is almost the entire population of Australia or Ghana!

Survivors may experience a great range of conflicting emotions about the deceased, feeling everything from intense sadness about the loss, helplessness to prevent it, longing for the person they lost, anger at the deceased for taking their own life to, sometimes, even relief.

Leroy Aarons' *Prayers for Bobby* - which became an Emmy-nominated Lifetime television movie - explores the transformation of Mary Griffith after her son Bobby commited suicide, and is an excellent study on the subject.

So far, the focus ends just on the person who died and the close survivors of the victim/ perpetrator. But what does that say about us, as a society, as a community? That was the source of my grief at Mass. In this instance, this was, to all intents and purposes, a godly and upright man, a regular at Mass. Where did all of that go in those final moments? Did our faith community become so good at imparting religion that it failed to instill faith? Did all of us, individuals, become so consumed with our own selves that we failed to see the hurt and broken body sitting right next to us in the pews? Have we, as a people, set so much store by maintaining the appearance of perfection that we, in effect, and without realizing it, turn up our noses at anything which might appear less than?

We have lost the ancient art of touch. We avoid any form of intimacy. We have built invisible bubbles that we travel in and function daily, our lives crisscrossing with others' too briefly, and not close enough to make any meaningful connections. We send text messages instead of calling. We are too self-absorbed to share a smile in the elevator or a simple "Good morning".

Do we have any idea whose day we might make with just a genuine look in the eye and a smile? There are too many people who feel alienated in our society; too many people who are invisible to us…but we are lost in our thoughts, too busy minding our own business or chasing after the next thing to even notice. And, sometimes, when we notice, we are too selfish to do anything about it.

We call it suicide, but I beg to differ. I call it murder. And we all are complicit in this crime. The verdict is in:

Guilty. Murder in the first.

# PERFECTION IS OVERRATED

*"Striving for excellence motivates you; striving for perfection is demoralizing."*

**- Harriet Braiker**

Trying to achieve perfection is like trying to be God.

As a producer and director of live shows and commercials at 24 years of age, I used to be what you would call a perfectionist. The shade of a color had to be exact; the crease on a drape would had to be just-so; the music had to be at a certain decibel level....

You can imagine how frustrated I became and how unhappy I could be, if the slightest nuance was anything other than I had imagined. A whole show could be ruined in my eyes because the host didn't reach the podium at the precise point I wanted in the music. It didn't matter to me that no one in the audience was aware that anything was gone awry.

And this is by no means an ode to mediocrity. I still abhor giving anything that is less than stellar. However, I have found that I can still have very high standards without sweating the small stuff.

Looking back I realize that my pursuit of perfection had nothing to do with what I perceived to be wrong, but what I perceived to be a reflection – or an extension – of my persona. I was trying to prove to myself and to everyone else that I was good enough. The words of the Broadway show *Dreamgirls* rings in my head: "*Mama said I've gotta prove that I am just as good; I'm even better than… Shine, Nina shine…*" I felt the only way to get noticed in a positive light was to be perfect, better than anyone else.

And I always fell short.

It's about balance and priorities. Some things are not worth the extra effort if its sole purpose is the achievement of perfection. If at a place-setting, the knife is placed half an inch too far away from the spoon, does it ruin the whole? Will agonizing over that imperfection change anything? Indeed, will making the adjustment add much more to the event? How many people will notice the subtle 'imperfection'? I had to learn what was important and what was not. I'd rather spend my time making sure that the food is at the right temperature and brought in on time and served right, than checking how many inches the knife is from the spoon...

Too many people accept mediocrity and that is wrong. But then an obsession for perfection is also wrong. I'm all for excellence, but I have learned that beyond a certain point, the law of diminishing returns sets in, and anything after that is a personal quest for the impossible, because perfection is a moving target. Trying to achieve perfection is like trying to be God. You can come awfully close to it, but you cannot be it. There isn't just a fine line between excellence and perfection - it's a chasm!

# OUR ELASTIC SPIRIT

*"My scars remind me that I did indeed survive my deepest wounds. That in itself is an accomplishment. And they bring to mind something else, too. They remind me that the damage life has inflicted on me has, in many places, left me stronger and more resilient. What hurt me in the past has actually made me better equipped to face the present."*

**— Steve Goodier**

Just the other day, I read an email from a reader named Kathie that deeply touched me and reaffirmed my belief in the strength of the human spirit. Even though we only communicated via email, the beauty of her spirit came through, and her story put both a tear in my eye and a smile on my face. With her permission, I share her story.

Kathie was born to a mother with substance abuse problems, and witnessed her mother battered. She herself was sexually abused between the ages of 3 and 7, was a victim of arson, then separated from her siblings and put up for foster care. She was eventually adopted when she was 11. We have heard many horror stories about how people who go through such harrowing experiences at a young age turn out. Not Kathie.

She wrote to me regarding my blog post on "Gratitude": *"...the two things that got me through these experiences are forgiveness and gratitude. Even as a child, it was in my DNA to understand that I needed to be grateful for these experiences - not only for the way in which they contributed to who I am today, but because they happened to me and not to someone who couldn't have handled them."*

This still makes my eyes well up. This is not just a true story of the attitude of gratitude, but also the triumph of the human spirit. This was the story of one woman who would not let the circumstances of her life situation dictate the trajectory of her life. It is all too easy to blame our life circumstances on our parents, or our tough life, or on someone who was unwilling to help, or some element of society conspiring against our success.

It takes a certain stoicism and resilience to push through all that, but it can be done. In an odd sort of way, on the other hand, it requires a peculiar vulnerability and acceptance of the situation, in the same way a reed is more likely to survive an intense storm than an oak tree is.

A little over five years ago, my life changed dramatically overnight and for a moment, I thought my life, as I knew it, was coming to an end. A few days later, after wading through the sea of my despair and confusion, and resolving to make the most of what life I had left, I had my most profound spiritual experience yet. I recall speaking to a psychologist friend and wondering whether I was okay: my exhilarating feeling of joy seemed terribly out of place in my circumstances. I had to know I wasn't losing my marbles! What happened was that I opened myself to peace once I stopped fighting and surrendered - hence my indescribable joy. I eventually realized that, ironically, small things get me more worked up than major life upheavals, once I discovered the strength in me. That is what brought me to this point.

Echoing what Kathie said to me in her email, if you are brought to the situation, you will be brought through the situation with the attitude of gratitude and a generous helping of forgiveness, even if it is only forgiving yourself. Like her, I have learnt that the human spirit is indomitable and incredibly elastic; bouncing back eventually and bouncing back stronger. Just like intense heat refines precious metals, intense situations refine precious spirits - yours included.

My sincere thanks to Kathie for inspiring this piece!

*"Resilience is accepting your new reality, even if it's less good than the one you had before. You can fight it, you can do nothing but scream about what you've lost, or you can accept that and try to put together something that's good."*

— Elizabeth Edwards

# FRIENDS & LOVERS

*"When we honestly ask ourselves which person in our lives mean the most to us, we often find that it is those who, instead of giving advice, solutions, or cures, have chosen rather to share our pain and touch our wounds with a warm and tender hand. The friend who can be silent with us in a moment of despair or confusion, who can stay with us in an hour of grief and bereavement, who can tolerate not knowing, not curing, not healing and face with us the reality of our powerlessness, that is a friend who cares."*

**- Henri J.M. Nouwen, The Road to Daybreak: A Spiritual Journey**


This is probably the longest chapter in the book, but I'm sure it will be worth the read...

### Third Culture Kid

After traveling to dozens of countries and living in half a dozen others, one of the issues I've constantly had to maneuver around has been that of friendship. I've had to manage making new friends in a new environment and maintaining old friends in other places. As a 'third culture kid' who is from everywhere and nowhere, I haven't had the luxury of friendships built on the comfort of constancy and longevity. In addition, the nuances of the concepts, responsibilities and expectations of friendships seem to vary by culture, age and outlook. Unfortunately, we only learn about friendship in the classroom of life, in the school of hard knocks.

## The Laws of Attraction

Most people include friends and family in the list of things that mean the most to them. But unlike family, which we don't choose, we do choose our friends and we could change friends if we wanted to. So what makes us talk to one of our classmates and not the other? And no, it doesn't 'just happen'. Much as we'd like to think we like our friends just for their sake, nothing could be farther from the truth.

At what point does a person make the transition from being an acquaintance to being a friend? It's not as though people have 'the conversation' about becoming friends. The laws of attraction in friendship are pretty similar to those of romantic relationships; and yes, there is an element of sexual attraction even for platonic friends! Our friends are people with whom we have shared interests or experiences; people who like what we like, have what have, or have what we would like to have. They also reflect us as individuals as well as in our social outlook. We would not have friends if we didn't derive some benefit from them.

## Cultural Differences

The Max Planck Institute for Human Development in Germany and the Chinese Academy of Sciences posed a scenario to children between 7 and 15: Each of them has promised to meet up with one of their old friends who's having problems, but a new classmate comes along later offering to take them to a concert, all expenses paid. How did they decide? Both sets of younger kids choose to go to the concert with the new friend but for different reasons. For the young Icelanders, it was friendship versus personal freedom and freedom won out. For the young Chinese, it was a choice between loyalty to old friends, or integrating a new kid into the social network. For the Chinese, either option was about putting the group first. For the older kids in the group, both Chinese and Icelanders chose to meet with the old friend – the Icelanders because they felt it was the right moral choice, and the Chinese because of the virtue of close friendship. So it is interesting how the concept of friendship changes, as we age, what culture we belong (or don't belong to) and according to our individual personalities.

Somehow I believe the all-encompassing Ghanaian concept of friendship resonated most with my personality style and structured my idea of how to relate to other people. For the Ghanaian, if you share a meal or drink together, if you invite or are invited to someone's home, you're no longer acquaintances. And Ghanaians did not earn the moniker 'Africa's friendliest people' on a whim: they are happy to welcome a stranger into their home anytime and will insist they share a meal with them. When I moved to the US, I had to adjust to the new concepts of personal space and privacy that to me, seemed to put up walls interfering with intimacy and spontaneous bonding. I was shocked that next door neighbors didn't know each other; it infuriated me that people in the elevator would not respond to a general greeting; it seemed silly to ask a good friend if it was ok to come over...

## We Have Ignition

So how does a friendship begin? In general, the transition point at which a casual acquaintance moves into the friend status is the point where either party discloses some rather personal information. As C.S. Lewis puts it in The Four Loves: *"Friendship is born at that moment when one person says to another: "What! You too? I thought that no one but myself . . .'"*

After my family moved to Ghana from Switzerland, I was made to sit in the front of the class for special attention. English was not my first language so I needed extra help in my third-grade class. With me at the front were Alemu, an

Ethiopian, and Alec, who became my best friend. Apart from sitting next to each other in class, Alec and I bonded because we both grew up in Europe and had similar sensibilities. We also both hated playing soccer (actually, we couldn't play even if our lives depended on it) and we both shared a love for aviation. As it happened, Alec's dad was a pilot. When Alec's family moved to the next street from me in our teenage years, we were inseparable. With Alec, our shared dislike for football (which we daren't share with anyone for fear of being labeled sissies) was just the beginning....

Being the kind of person that I am, I get people opening up to me sometimes within minutes of meeting, sometimes in spite of their better judgment. But then I probably invite that in a subtle way by consciously conveying the sense of a safe space to confide in – sometimes by opening up first. Being vulnerable gives others permission to be vulnerable as well. Somehow, self-disclosure is an indicator that the person trusts you enough to share a personal part of their story with you – and instinctively we feel elevated to a different level of relationship. That, in turn, prompts us to self-disclose as well, cementing the sense of a shared bond.

## It's A Two-Way Street Or The Long Goodnight

Reciprocation is also necessary to keep the balance of a friendship going. A few years ago, a good friend of mine and I would talk very frequently, even when I moved out of state. At a point our conversations centered on his new, but turbulent relationship.

Occasionally, he'd remember to ask how I was doing and I'd start telling him and he'd often take the conversation back to his situation. I eventually resorted to just giving brief platitudes because I felt he wasn't listening and he wouldn't notice, anyway. As his relationship improved, I got fewer and fewer calls; my calls were returned less frequently and our interactions fizzled out to the point where I only call on birthdays and holidays. The lack of reciprocation diluted the strength of the friendship. It is the intuitive understanding of keeping balance in a relationship that makes friendships thrive.

No one likes an opinionated friend. A friend who always thinks your choices are wrong will be a friend you'd love to avoid. A friend of mine, who shall remain nameless, had very rigid ideas about what I should be doing or had to believe in. Their religious beliefs had to be mine; their way of driving had to be mine; their leisure choices had to be mine. Needless to say, I can only have them in small doses. But, I must say, and in keeping with being a real friend, I have made my feelings known to them in an honest, non-accusing and loving way. To their credit, they are more conscious of it now.

## Surviving In The Trenches

The building blocks of mutually satisfying, long-lasting close friendships include unquestioning acceptance, unconditional support, staying positive, loyalty, trust and honesty. Thankfully, proximity is not essential for friendship to thrive, but staying in touch is: call, visit, text, email…something, anything…. But the cement that holds all of these together is a combination of a well-developed sense of intimacy and emotional expressiveness.

A good friend knows exactly what to say at the right time…or when not to say anything at all. A good friend is one in whose presence you can cry and be vulnerable without being concerned about being composed. A good friend knows instinctively when you just want to vent and understands that you don't need them to give you advice or try to fix a situation. It isn't the friend who lends us a couple of bucks – or a couple hundred – when we're in a bind; or the one who picks us up from the airport that we treasure most. It is the one with the emotional prowess that leaves an indelible mark on our hearts. That is why we can't pay our way through friendship. Unless we really invest emotionally into our friendships, the ones we have will remain shallow and lack longevity.

*"The glory of friendship is not the outstretched hand, nor the kindly smile, nor the joy of companionship; it's the spiritual inspiration that comes to one when he discovers that someone else believes in him and is willing to trust him with his friendship".*

- Ralph Waldo Emerson

## Moving On Up

But the elite status of 'best friend' is another kettle of fish altogether. It's like friendship on steroids and the responsibilities and expectations are much higher. Our best friend is the one we expect to pick up the phone when we call at 4:00 in the morning. Our best friend is the one we know will leave everything to be beside us when we suffer a loss. However, the one element that separates a best friend from our other friends is that a best friend supports and reflects our social identity. We may have friends from all walks of life, but our best friend affirms our primary social identity – mother, mechanic, socialite, fashionista, jock… We naturally gravitate towards people who support our view of ourselves. And when our identity changes, our friends may change as well. The relationship I had with Alec changed when he got married – not in a bad way – but the dynamic changed. He was married and I wasn't. We stay in touch and I am very close with his wife, but life happened. Marriage, divorce, parenthood and change in lifestyle will do that.

## That's What Friends Are For

To be loved, one must first start by being lovable. To have good friends, one must start by being a good friend. I happen to believe that no one crosses the path of my life by accident. Some will leave footsteps on my heart long after they've moved on; some came in just to teach me a lesson or to teach me something about myself. Whatever the case may be, I am grateful for the people who have made the tapestry of my life as rich as it is today.

I don't take friendships lightly and I hold dear all the friends I've made around the world. To every single one of you – and you know who you are – this is dedicated to you. I hope I've been as good a friend to you as you have been to me.

# ON PREJUDICE AND FEAR

*"We cannot trample upon the humanity of others without devaluing our own. The Igbo, always practical, put it concretely in their proverb* Onyeji onye n'ani ji onwe ya: *'He who will hold another down in the mud must stay in the mud to keep him down'".*

**- Chinua Achebe, The Education of a British-Protected Child: Essays**

Permit me to get on a soapbox today. I just watched a TV series that rubbed me the wrong way and for all the wrong reasons. There was nothing wrong in anyway with the episode I watched, except that, as art imitating life, it put into perspective one of my pet peeves.

Part of the episode included the beating of a young man by three other males because he was gay and how the young man's four friends each reacted to the startling reminder of their vulnerability. I felt a mélange of emotions so raw I surprised myself, since I am not given to particularly strong emotions. I felt deep sorrow, seething rage, utter disgust and a primal urge to scream, despite my rationalizing that it was just a TV show.

Violence of any sort upsets me. Violence against any kind of minority enrages me. Regarding this TV show episode, the person who was beaten (I refuse to use the word 'victim'), was minding his own business at a gas station and made no threatening gestures; used no threatening words. So why was he attacked?

But much as we would like to wish the perpetrators away as some misguided, ignorant individuals who couldn't possibly be counted among our upstanding and enlightened circle of friends, I beg to differ. Those three men represent us in some form or fashion, to some degree. It may not be expressed as outwardly or violently, and it may not be against gay people, but we look at people who are different from us in some way, through the prism of our prejudice. And prejudice is a result of ignorance. Unfortunately, even religions adopt an "us-versus-them" attitude.

We hurt people in subtle ways because of their skin color, hair color, height, race, religious beliefs, sexual orientation and identity, their bank accounts (or lack thereof), their size and a host of other factors. The absence of action is, in itself, an action. You may not go around bashing people physically, but are you doing anything to make things better? Are we so insecure about ourselves that we have to bring others down to feel better about ourselves and the safe, little, artificial cocoons we have created for ourselves? Again it all boils down to fear. Our prejudices reflect our own fears: our fear of being fat, or poor, or black or gay, or white. Our prejudices also project our smug arrogance and self-righteousness.

*"The test of courage comes when we are in the minority. The test of tolerance comes when we are in the majority."*

\- Ralph W. Sockman

As one who has lived in and visited many countries, and as one who has been on both sides of the minority-majority divide, I know that we all want the same things. We all want to love and be loved, whether we are the oppressors or the oppressed, yet we cannot see beyond our noses to find the inextricable bond that we share. One of my favorite songs is *Colors of the Wind*, from Disney's Pocahontas, and my favorite verse there goes:

*"You think the only people who are people*
*Are the people who look and think like you*
*But if you walk the footsteps of a stranger,*
*You'll learn things you never knew you never knew..."*

If there is one thing I've learned in 40 years, it is tolerance. Let's make a pact today to teach our kids to be tolerant. The world doesn't need any more hatred of any sort. In the words of Rodney King:

*"Can we all get along?"* A difference in opinion or perspective on life is not equivalent to being an enemy. Remember the Golden Rule: *Do unto others as you would have them do unto you.*

I will now get off my soapbox.

*When the Nazis came for the communists,*
*I remained silent; I was not a communist.*
*When they locked up the socialists*
*I remained silent; I was not a socialist.*
*When they came for the trade unionists,*
*I did not speak out; I was not a trade unionist.*
*When they came for the Jews, I remained silent;*
*I wasn't a Jew.*
*When they came for me,*
*there was no one left to speak out.*

‐ Martin Niemöller

# SMILE, YOU'RE ON LIFE!

*Smile though your heart is aching*

*Smile even though it's breaking*

*When there are clouds in the sky, you'll get by*

*If you smile through your fear and sorrow*

*Smile and maybe tomorrow*

*You'll see the sun come shining through for you...*

**- Nat King Cole**

Joy and pain are two feelings that are understood just about anywhere in the world. A subset of joy is the smile - a simple facial expression that shows happiness, pleasure or amusement.

After traveling to dozens of countries in four continents, I can confidently say that barring some cultural nuances, a smile is generally internationally understood and acknowledged. Smile, and, indeed, the world smiles with you.

As a store clerk at a major retailer during one of my 'dark' phases some years ago, it was a daily struggle just to go to work. With multiple degrees, I was working a minimum-wage job and depressed. I used to savor the last moments in my car before I clocked in for work because, once I opened the

121

door, I'd have to leave my problems there and don my smile. Many times, customers would remark about how chipper I was, what a dazzling smile I had; how much fun I was having. My work ethic was such that I had to dig deep and 'switch it on' for the duration of my shift. I had to be the best at what I did, no matter how lowly it was.

In some way, when a customer smiled back or responded to my good vibe, it made me feel better. What they wouldn't know is that I hated my job, I was depressed, my feet were aching from walking five miles and standing, or that the arthritis in my back made me want to scream… The moment I walked out of those doors at the end of my shift, I would feel the drain wash over me like a ponderous wave. I was spent but glad I'd given it my all.

I have seen how people are positively affected by a simple smile. There've been times I have flashed a smile to a surly waiter or receptionist and gotten better service. A smile announces that you bring good energy and a positive spirit.

But a smile is good for us as well. I can only speak from experience, but I'm sure many can relate. A smile puts me in a good mood if I'm able to push through what I'm feeling. I've been told by some that they find my smile attractive (I say 'thank you'). We are all attracted to people who smile, and a smile actually makes you more attractive - and that goes a long way in boosting sex appeal! Scientists also say it helps your immune system, lowers your blood pressure, relieves stress, and all sorts of other good stuff. Now, if those aren't good enough reasons, smiling actually makes you appear more confident and successful....

So, before you get out of bed tomorrow, put a smile on your face. And throughout your day smile some more to look younger, feel younger and live longer - it couldn't hurt - and put a smile on someone else's face!

# SEEING THROUGH ROSE-COLORED GLASSES

*"You can't be alive if you are living in fear, and if you're living in fear you can't see and experience life; the magnificence of your life that is right in front of you in each moment."*

**- Daisetsu Teitaro Suzuki**

Sometimes when we feel like we are at the lowest points in our life, it seems impossible to be grateful for anything. How can anyone find anything good about misfortune or tragedy?

I quit a job I hated to change the trajectory of my career. I went back to school full time, graduated valedictorian with long list of awards, and incurred an immense amount of debt. Eighteen months later, with no job, no home, mounting debt, battling depression, barely surviving on welfare and hopping from one friend's couch to another, I often asked myself "What do I have to be grateful for?"

Japanese author Daisetsu Teitaro Suzuki writes of a Zen teacher telling the story of a monk who was being chased by a tiger and climbs over the edge of a cliff, hanging on a vine to avoid the tiger. Looking down, the monk finds many more tigers down below waiting to pounce on him if he landed.

Caught almost literally between a rock and a hard place, he sees a strawberry on the vine, smiles, and thankfully reaches out and pops the strawberry in his mouth.

What has the strawberry got to do with the danger the monk was in? Nothing and everything. What it tells us is that the monk was living in the moment. He was not so consumed by the danger that lay before or behind him that the strawberry became insignificant. He was present enough to notice the ripe juiciness of the strawberry. He didn't lose his appetite over his danger.

That's what gratitude does. Gratitude is like a pair of spectacles we wear that help us focus on what we have and blurs out what we don't have. It opens our eyes to see that there always is something to be thankful for.

I haven't always seen things that way in my times of despair, but when I have practiced having the attitude of gratitude I have seen the results in amazing ways. My problems have seemed to recede into the background and I have been able to be present and enjoy my moments.

More than once I've been asked, "How do you manage?" I am blessed with great friends who have opened their homes to me. I have been blessed with the taking away of material possessions so I can see what truly matters. I go to bed each night grateful for a roof over my head, just enough food to keep me going yet keep me hungry, family and friends that love me, and another day in Paradise.

Do I have it all figured out? Not by a long shot! I still have days where I feel miserable. I still have days when I feel the world is against me, when I just feel like stepping off the train of life for a moment and checking out for a bit. But when I go to bed, there's always the hope that joy will come in the morning. And I see the Cheshire cat in my mind's eye and I know that he's grinning that knowing grin....

Holding on to what's wrong in your current life situation (not your life), is like having a clenched fist. You cannot accept any goodness because you're closed. Gratitude is like letting go and opening up. In that moment you become alive, open to all the amazing sensations and nuances of your life.

From the Zen teacher's perspective in Suzuki's story, *"You can't be alive if you are living in fear, and if you're living in fear you can't see and experience life; the magnificence of your life that is right in front of you in each moment."*

# LET'S HAVE A KIKI!

*"... A kiki is a party, for calming all your nerves*

*We're spilling tea, and dishing just desserts one may deserve*

*And though the sun is rising, few may choose to leave*

*So shade that lid and we'll all bid adieu to your ennui...*

*Let's have a kiki, I wanna have a kiki*

*Lock the doors, tight..."*

**- The Scissor Sisters**

As one who loves to entertain, I often detach myself from my duties as host and watch my guests interact, laugh and have a good time. Yes, the cleanup is always a drag, but the headiness of a pleasure-filled gathering always brings me back for more.

A party, for me, does not conjure up woebegone images of hard work, dirty dishes, and a tornado-swept home. For me, it's an opportunity to create a fun experience that I can manage. There's nothing more enjoyable than seeing and hearing the oohs and aahs of guests as you unveil one little surprise here and another one there. Otherwise, just the sense of relaxation and peace that radiates from guests at intimate gatherings is priceless.

129

It is fascinating to watch how our lives are inextricably linked, one to another, and there is great joy and reward in bringing people together. At social gatherings, people share many things, and relationships are strengthened and new ones are made.

I have learnt that I can facilitate positive change in people's lives in my one-on-one interactions with them, as well as by creating a safe and welcoming space where people come to share joy that they can go and share with others in turn. It's a gift that keeps on giving.

What is even better is that it is in giving that we receive. The joy of giving is in the joy we receive. I often have an out of body experience during such gatherings, just watching everything with a smile. Life is good.

*"Let us eat, drink, and be merry for tomorrow we'll die"*
- Isaiah 22:13

# BEYOND BIRTHDAY SUITS

*"I believe that fashion is not about what you wear, but how you wear it. It's more than putting together outfits and creating different looks, but a form of expression of one's identity, creating a new outer layer of skin."*

**- Adetayo Fajemisin**

In our somewhat warped way of thinking, we tend to get a feel of other people - especially people we don't know - based on their outward appearances. On the one hand, this might seem subjective, but our brains have to have a way of filtering the information we receive in order to categorize and simplify it. So we put new people we meet into various categories and file them in the cavernous storage systems of our mind. As a result we have a host of idioms that point to that, such as: "Clothes make the man", and "You only have one chance to make a good first impression".

Many years ago, as a very young and hands-on event producer/director, I would be in the trenches with the crew and various vendors, dressed in old jeans, sneakers and t-shirt. I asked an employee of one of the vendors I had contracted if I could borrow his ladder for a moment and I got a rude retort from him. Some time later, I saw the manager of the vending company and recounted the story to her and she was terribly embarrassed and furious, "Does he know who you are?" she fumed. Apparently not, but that isn't the point. The point is that I did not fit into his category of what a director should look like. I was dressed like the rest of them, was too young, wasn't shouting orders, didn't elicit any fear from the crew and didn't approach him with a sense of entitlement. I thought it quite funny when I later got a rather sheepish apology from him because I understood what had happened.

But watching what you wear is not just about making an impression for other peoples' benefit. What you wear has an effect on how you feel about yourself and even how you move. The way I carry myself in a suit is quite different from the way I carry myself in shorts and flip-flops. On days I'm not feeling too upbeat, dressing extra dapper than usual with a splash of color usually does the trick. It really is a two-pronged effect: I feel better about myself and people respond more warmly to me, which makes me feel even better!

So Mum was right: press your shirts, polish your shoes, tuck your shirt in, brush you hair...and the world is a better and more beautiful place.

# EXPLORE. DREAM. DISCOVER.

*Twenty years from now you'll be more disappointed by the things that you didn't do than by the ones you did. So throw off the bowlines. Sail away from the harbor. Catch the trade winds in your sails. Explore. Dream. Discover.*

**- Mark Twain**

I've heard people say you should try something new everyday. I've never been good at keeping track of that, or, more importantly, making that happen. I do, however, try to have a totally new experience every now and then. This month, I want to learn scuba diving - thank goodness for options like Groupon and LivingSocial. Last month, I went parasailing. Again. I'd love to go swimming with sharks.

Ever wondered why as you grow older, time seems to go faster and faster? A very interesting correlation has been found between having new experiences - or the lack thereof - and one's perception of the passage of time. When you surround yourself with the familiar and remain within your comfort zone, the brain doesn't need to do much work. It quickly processes the information and moves on. When new information is received, it has to process the new information, which slows it down - and slows down your perception of time. A quote from David Eagleman, a neuroscientist who studies the effects of the brain's perception of time, summarizes it well: "The more familiar the world becomes, the less information your brain writes down, and the more quickly time seems to pass. Time is this rubbery thing...it stretches out when you really turn your brain resources on, and when you say, 'Oh, I got this, everything is as expected,' it shrinks up."

(I recommend Adam Dachis' post: *Why New Experiences Are Important and How They Positively Affect Your Perception of Time* for a short read, but if you have time you will find *The Possibilian*, a profile of David Eagleman, extremely fascinating.)

A new experience doesn't have to be some dramatic new event that shakes your world in ways you never thought possible. It could be driving down a road in a direction you've never explored before; trying a cuisine that you haven't thought to try before; attending a class to learn something new, trying a crossword puzzle, or walking on the treadmill backwards! Actually, a simple action like walking backwards can help improve your memory skills...go figure.

So go on, try something new and get a grip on the reins of time. And while you're at it, remember to enjoy the experience. Go ahead!

# RECHARGE & RELOAD

*"Go placidly amid the noise and haste and remember what peace there may be in silence..."*

**- Max Erhmann, The Desiderata**

I was surprised to find out in a yoga class how much I was NOT breathing. Of course, I breathe, thought I - I don't even have to think about it. But that was the problem, I realized. I was so consumed with everyday living that I failed to notice that my breathing had become more shallow over the years.

If you watch a baby breathing, they take deep breaths and fill their lungs with air and release. As humans, we are hard-wired to have a fight or flight reaction to any stressors and our breathing becomes more shallow as a result. As we grow older, and with more stressors, our breathing gets less and less relaxed. This means less oxygen to the blood and the body has to work harder, putting even more stress on it, and we get ill as a result. A lot of heart diseases could be averted with proper breathing techniques. Deep breathing increases the oxygen intake and slows down the heart rate.

But this is not just about the action of breathing. It really is about slowing down. We live in such an 'instamatic' world that everything needs to be done better and faster. We are moving through this world at dizzying speeds with nary a pause for a swig of water or a tire change. We work longer days than we did 50 years ago; we are bombarded by a myriad stimuli every waking moment, and because everything moves so much faster, we try to get a lot more into each day.

I've learnt that sometimes we all need to renew our spirit. Take time to really breathe; smell the roses; meditate - whatever name you choose to call it. The opening line of Max Ehrmann's Desiderata - one of the most succinct guides for living - says: *"Go placidly amid the noise and haste and remember what peace there may be in silence..."*

# GETTING TO HAPPY

*"Happiness cannot be traveled to, owned, earned, worn or consumed. Happiness is the spiritual experience of living every minute with love, grace, and gratitude."*

**- Denis Waitley**

It's very easy to get swamped by the many distractions that make up our lives in the modern world. Our hectic lives have become more outward-oriented and we are soon enveloped by a swarm of activities and thoughts and worries, and…. well, you get the picture.

I get that way in my life too when there's a lot going on and I'm buzzing around for all the world like a hummingbird on speed. Then I begin to feel the weight of the world, and begin to sink into misery, overwhelmed, dizzy, and out of the flow.

Thankfully, there are some ways to get ourselves back in kilter and help make our lives a bit more tolerable. I'm sure that given enough time, I could come up with hundred of things that would help – and I am certain you could, as well. Here are just five that I thought of.

**See a different perspective.** I've always said that nothing we experience is inherently good or bad. They take on a good or bad hue, depending on how we see them, and which side of the equation we are on. So, for instance, we would consider a death a tragedy, but for the undertaker, it's more business. Rain might be a nuisance when you have to be outdoors, but the farmer is delighted with the rain that makes his crops grow. But that is oversimplifying the issue. When we are able to see life events as neutral, not as events designed to make us miserable, we are able to keep up a positive attitude to deal with them. That in itself makes life more tolerable…making us less unhappy. In other words, have an attitude of gratitude.

**Be content.** I have come to realize that I can be content with having nothing more than a few old clothes and nowhere to call my own. Much of the world's unhappiness comes from not being content with what we have. We are happy with a $10,000 increase in our paycheck until we become aware that someone else got a $12,000 increase. Our car is fine until we see someone pull up in a sleek Mercedes. This is not to say ambition is wrong - on the contrary, ambition is great, but we will enjoy what we have better if we spent less time pining for, and desiring what we don't have or can't have.

**Try something new.** In earlier chapters, I wrote about how trying new experiences can keep you young, and how money can buy you happiness. It is experiences, not material wealth that makes us happy. It is having the experience of something different that makes us feel awesome.

**Make love often.** Sex – especially the good kind – releases endorphins and serotonin, which create the feel-good sensation and the DHEA hormone, which helps circulation. It also relaxes muscles and releases you of stress. Indeed, if there was ever a fountain of youth, it would be healthy sexual intimacy. Regular sex can shave off 4-7 years off your age! What's not to love? Need I say more?

**Give more. Expect less.** Think of everything you do as intending to be beneficial. How does what you do help someone else? Remember, what goes around comes around. Imagine all the good karma that comes back to you from the good you do…. Once you get into the habit of doing good for goodness' sake, expecting less will follow naturally. When you expect less, you experience less disappointment. Less disappointment mean less energy spent on being upset and more energy for being happy.

**Live in the now.** It is difficult to focus on the good things happening to us right now, when we are fixated on what could happen or what happened in the past. Everything happens in the present. Not in the past or the future. We spend our energies clinging to the memory of what happened, or creating an illusion of what might happen before it actually does. In the meantime, the beauty of what is happening right here, right now, is totally lost on us: the soft breeze, the birds chirping, the whiff of fragrance from a flower, a baby crying in the distance....

By living a simpler life, we cut down on the worries as well, making it easier for us to move our outward focus more inward. Let's not go too long only to realize that what we were looking for out there, was really in here all along....

# REINVENT YOUR STORY

*"I believe in the complexity of the human story and that there's no way you can tell that story in one way and say, 'This is it'. Always there will be someone who can tell it differently depending on where they are standing; the same person telling the story will tell it differently."*

**- Chinua Achebe**

A conversation with a friend of mine yesterday got me thinking about all the jobs I've worked at in my life, and especially the ones that do not show up on my resume. A hodgepodge of varied - usually menial - jobs that have added to the richness of the tapestry of my life.

In the summer of 1983, my father lost his job as a diplomat in Ghana's foreign service following the military coup d'état of 1981, just before his next scheduled posting. Announced on the radio for all the world to hear, my father lost his job, we lost our status and our place in life, that year of El Niño and drought around the world. That began our sojourn in the land of borderline poverty that would last more than a decade. But for the grace of owning our home, we could have ended up homeless and destitute.

But my family is as resilient as we are close, and with hindsight, I realize how my brothers and I developed an enterprising spirit and the ability to re-invent our stories. Over the course of our years of dearth, we did anything and everything we could to make ends meet. As the eldest of my parents' kids, the lot fell to me to me to be involved with the development and implementation of all of these ideas.

One of the many activities we did was producing plantain chips for distribution to stores. I'd go with my mother to the central market where all the market vendors would gather to bargain for their supplies. We'd buy bunches of plantains and have the market carriers get them to the car, balancing their unwieldy loads on their heads. Back at the house, we'd immediately get to the task of peeling the hundreds of fingers of plantain while the large pot of oil was getting hot. Peeling green plantains can be taxing on one's thumbs and even painful at times. The sap from the thick skin of the plantains was also almost impossible to get off, turning a reddish-brown from a colorless state.

My father also tried farming - a far cry from being the high-level diplomat and foreign policy maker. We would travel deep in the countryside of Ghana, buying cassava (yucca) from the local farmers and bringing them to the city to sell to the market women. My father, using his well-developed chameleon-like people skills quickly developed relationships with both the farmers and the market women, and was always greeted enthusiastically whenever *Forgive and Forget* showed up. (Forgive and Forget was the inscription on the old, rickety, converted ambulance that we chartered for these runs.)

The rice paddy fizzled out before it really had a chance, but the okra farming was probably the worst. At harvest time, we'd be on the farm at the crack of dawn to get as much work in before the midday sun reached its scorching peak. The hairs on the okra would prick my young fingers and stick there for hours after that. Ouch!

The poultry farm was fun. Not. Everything about it smelled awful. We'd pick their eggs twice a day, and feed them, change their water and give them vitamins. Once a week we'd change the sawdust - stinky! Depending on the orders we had to supply restaurants and hotels, we'd have to slaughter and dress some birds. (Don't worry - I will not go into the gory details of that process here.) It's easy to take for granted the processes that have to happen before the chicken appears in the freezer of your grocery.

Prior to that, I'd never killed a chicken before and I haven't since. Believe it or not, I was actually afraid of chickens! I was able to be great at it because of a certain detachment, and it was an assembly-line environment and I just did what I had to do. Everyone in the family did their part and we never complained.

At one point, for some reason that still eludes me, my father - bless his soul - decided to try his hands at woodworking. With our circular saw, lathe, sander and other accoutrements in tow and hardly a crash course in woodworking, we would go round doing minor home improvement projects for clients. We eventually contracted a carpenter to help out with larger projects, but that didn't leave much money for us.

Oh, and there was the aluminum pot sand-casting business. It involved buying and smelting aluminum ingots and pouring them into casts. Once it was set, we'd break open the casts and sand down the pots. These pots were bought and used by the local food restaurants called chop bars for large batches of cooking over open-hearth fires.

Then my mother, who had been a teacher, decided to open a crèche and nursery for infants 3 months to three years old. Thus began the decade of changing diapers, burping, bottle feeding and soothing crying babies. We gave up our living room and dining room to make room for cots, playpens, play areas and eating tables. Having the experience of caring for my younger brothers, I was a natural, and for some reason, I happen to be good at calming babies. My mom was 'Mummy' to all the kids and my brother was 'Daddy' to them - his specialty was fooling around and playing horse games with the kids. It's no wonder my youngest brother is turning out to be an amazing dad himself....

There were many weekends when we were catching our breath from juggling a school of loud, attention-seeking babies when there would be a knock at the door - a parent with their kid who was crying because they wanted to go to 'Mummy'. It didn't matter that they were with their own 'Mummy'; they wanted 'the other Mummy'... Of course, we kept a 'no kid turned away' policy, so they'd stay over for a few hours while their parents enjoyed the weekend!

I didn't mention our attempt at fish farming, and digging up the backyard for a fish pond, or the computer school in our garage, the consignment of white cement that turned out to be nothing more than carbide, the fish distribution service, cooking kenkey (a steamed staple made from corn dough akin to tamales) or the many other enterprises we tried. With every failure, we learned what didn't work.

They were the worst jobs I ever loved....

My father eventually became the Registrar at the new University College of Education, which he helped set up. It was his last job.

I am immensely proud of my family - rallying together in sorrow and in joy. I remember how happy we were when we bought a television after more than 10 years of being without one. In place of a television, we would sit around at the end of the day and recount the funniest highlights of that day, tease each other and make up stories. Getting that television symbolized, for us, the beginning of our changing fortunes; the moment when we could actually save up to buy something as non-essential as a television.

Most people only see a well-educated, well-traveled, arbiter of style and assume I've had an upper-class life of privilege, wealth and influence. But that doesn't tell the whole story.

As individuals and as a family, we have become masters of re-creation, adept at rolling with the punches, getting up and dusting off ourselves. We have learnt first-hand that after you fall seven times, it isn't time to give up, but time to get up the eighth time!

And when the sun rises tomorrow, get up, get dressed, and show up for life.

# EPILOGUE

*"Owning our story can be hard but not nearly as difficult as spending our lives running from it. Embracing our vulnerabilities is risky but not nearly as dangerous as giving up on love and belonging and joy — the experiences that make us the most vulnerable. Only when we are brave enough to explore the darkness will we discover the infinite power of our light."*

**- Brené Brown**

Vulnerability is a terrifying notion to most. Being vulnerable strips us of our perceived defenses, but it gives us a lot more power than we credit it for.

In writing this book, I have had to face my fear of being vulnerable squarely. To be able to connect with you, I had to be honest. To be honest, I had to show not just the clean, pristine parts of my life, but also the gritty (read 'embarrassing') parts of my life. I had to let go of my perception of what other people's perception of me was. I had to recognize that my life circumstance is not a summation or essence of my life. But just as pain is the bedfellow of joy, every chapter of the book ended on a good note. The pain was only an enriching part of the process to a new high point and had to be celebrated. The pain was merely a means to an end.

*"To love at all is to be vulnerable. Love anything, and your heart will certainly be wrung and possibly be broken. If you want to make sure of keeping it intact, you must give your heart to no one, not even to an animal. Wrap it carefully round with hobbies and little luxuries; avoid all entanglements; lock it up safe in the casket or coffin of your selfishness. But in that casket — safe, dark, motionless, airless — it will change. It will not be broken; it will become unbreakable, impenetrable, irredeemable."*

— C.S. Lewis

As human beings, our two main motivating forces are love and fear and the strongest kinds of love are arguably motherly love and romantic love. But it is precisely love and fear that threaten to expose our vulnerability. To face fear and to experience love authentically we cannot but give in to vulnerability!

Think of vulnerability as a doorway to life. Surely, opening that door exposes us to pain. But that is the only way joy, love and the full experience of life can come in. So shall we lock out feeling, for fear of the possibility of hurt, when the only way to experience authenticity and love is through pain? Life is a 'twofer' package deal — you can't have one without the other. It's all or nothing.

The process of writing this book not only provided me perspective and a means of cathartic expression – it actually saved my life. It is a theme that keeps recurring in my writing and in a weird way I think I am slightly behind the curve of my own writing! But that is what I love about vulnerability: I don't have to be perfect and that's okay by me. I might have some pithy observations, but I don't have all the answers – I'm a work in progress myself. It is in some of my most vulnerable moments that I have some of my greatest inspirations. Creativity has a life of its own and cannot be made into what it's not.

*"We cultivate love when we allow our most vulnerable and powerful selves to be deeply seen and known, and when we honor the spiritual connection that grows from that offering with trust, respect, kindness and affection...Shame, blame, disrespect, betrayal, and the withholding of affection damage the roots from which love grows. Love can only survive these injuries if they are acknowledged, healed and rare."*

- Brené Brown, *The Gifts of Imperfection: Let Go of Who You Think You're Supposed to Be and Embrace Who You Are*

As I write the last chapter of this book, I am cognizant of the fact that I have shared parts of my life with you and shown the world how imperfect I am. I would be dishonest to say it doesn't terrify the living daylights out of me, but I am also aware of the love and acceptance I receive. Besides, being me is not contingent on what the world thinks of me and I have enjoyed the roller-coaster ride.

I am not trying to be perfect. Just awesome.

# ABOUT THE AUTHOR

R. Ayité Okyne is considered a true citizen of the world. He comes from a long line of African royalty and diplomats, has lived in six countries on four continents and speaks six languages. His international worldview affords him a unique perspective on the difficult and often complex interactions between peoples of different cultures.

With his broad exposure to different experiences, Ayité is able to bring to his writing a non-judgmental and approachable perspective. His writing challenges people to view life's situations in a different way, and guides them to find fresh perspectives they might otherwise have never thought of.

Ayité is a writer, lifestyle blogger, event producer, TV show host, public speaker and social commentator. He resides in both the United States and Ghana and has many interests including aviation, horseback riding, cooking and entertaining.

www.ayiteokyne.com

www.ingramcontent.com/pod-product-compliance
Lightning Source LLC
Chambersburg PA
CBHW070958040426
42443CB00007B/570